Business Weekly Planner Pages

for the
Organized Professional

Activinotes

Activinotes

DAILY JOURNALS, PLANNERS, NOTEBOOKS AND OTHER BLANK BOOKS

Weekly Planner

Monday

Tuesday

Wednesday

Thursday

Note

Friday

Saturday

Sunday

Weekly meeting

Clients to call

Things to prepare for next week

Weekly Planner

Monday

Tuesday

Wednesday

Thursday

Friday

Saturday

Sunday

Note

Weekly meeting

Clients to call

Things to prepare for next week

Weekly Planner

Monday

Tuesday

Wednesday

Thursday

Note

Friday

Saturday

Sunday

Weekly meeting

Clients to call

Things to prepare for next week

Weekly Planner

Monday

Tuesday

Wednesday

Thursday

Note

Friday

Saturday

Sunday

Weekly meeting

Clients to call

Things to prepare for next week

Weekly Planner

Monday

Tuesday

Wednesday

Thursday

Note

Friday

Saturday

Sunday

Weekly meeting

Clients to call

Things to prepare for next week

Weekly Planner

Monday

Tuesday

Wednesday

Thursday

Note

Friday

Saturday

Sunday

Weekly meeting

Clients to call

Things to prepare for next week

Weekly Planner

Monday

Tuesday

Wednesday

Thursday

Note

Friday

Saturday

Sunday

Weekly meeting

Clients to call

Things to prepare for next week

Weekly Planner

Monday

Tuesday

Wednesday

Thursday

Note

Friday

Saturday

Sunday

Weekly meeting

Clients to call

Things to prepare for next week

Weekly Planner

Monday

Tuesday

Wednesday

Thursday

Friday

Saturday

Sunday

Note

Weekly meeting

Clients to call

Things to prepare for next week

Weekly Planner

Monday

Tuesday

Wednesday

Thursday

Note

Friday

Saturday

Sunday

Weekly meeting

Clients to call

Things to prepare for next week

Weekly Planner

Monday

Tuesday

Wednesday

Thursday

Note

Friday

Saturday

Sunday

Weekly meeting

Clients to call

Things to prepare for next week

Weekly Planner

Monday

Tuesday

Wednesday

Thursday

Note

Friday

Saturday

Sunday

Weekly meeting

Clients to call

Things to prepare for next week

Weekly Planner

Monday

Tuesday

Wednesday

Thursday

Note

Friday

Saturday

Sunday

Weekly meeting

Clients to call

Things to prepare for next week

Weekly Planner

Monday

Tuesday

Wednesday

Thursday

Note

Friday

Saturday

Sunday

Weekly meeting

Clients to call

Things to prepare for next week

Weekly Planner

Monday

Tuesday

Wednesday

Thursday

Note

Friday

Saturday

Sunday

Weekly meeting

Clients to call

Things to prepare for next week

Weekly Planner

Monday

Tuesday

Wednesday

Thursday

Note

Friday

Saturday

Sunday

Weekly meeting

Clients to call

Things to prepare for next week

Weekly Planner

Monday

Tuesday

Wednesday

Thursday

Note

Friday

Saturday

Sunday

Weekly meeting

Clients to call

Things to prepare for next week

Weekly Planner

Monday

Tuesday

Wednesday

Thursday

Note

Friday

Saturday

Sunday

Weekly meeting

Clients to call

Things to prepare for next week

Weekly Planner

Monday

Tuesday

Wednesday

Thursday

Note

Friday

Saturday

Sunday

Weekly meeting

Clients to call

Things to prepare for next week

Weekly Planner

Monday

Tuesday

Wednesday

Thursday

Note

Friday

Saturday

Sunday

Weekly meeting

Clients to call

Things to prepare for next week

Weekly Planner

Monday

Tuesday

Wednesday

Thursday

Note

Friday

Saturday

Sunday

Weekly meeting

Clients to call

Things to prepare for next week

Weekly Planner

Monday

Tuesday

Wednesday

Thursday

Note

Friday

Saturday

Sunday

Weekly meeting

Clients to call

Things to prepare for next week

Weekly Planner

Monday

Tuesday

Wednesday

Thursday

Note

Friday

Saturday

Sunday

Weekly meeting

Clients to call

Things to prepare for next week

Weekly Planner

Monday

Tuesday

Wednesday

Thursday

Note

Friday

Saturday

Sunday

Weekly meeting

Clients to call

Things to prepare for next week

Weekly Planner

Monday

Tuesday

Wednesday

Thursday

Note

Friday

Saturday

Sunday

Weekly meeting

Clients to call

Things to prepare for next week

Weekly Planner

Monday

Tuesday

Wednesday

Thursday

Note

Friday

Saturday

Sunday

Weekly meeting

Clients to call

Things to prepare for next week

Weekly Planner

Monday

Tuesday

Wednesday

Thursday

Note

Friday

Saturday

Sunday

Weekly meeting

Clients to call

Things to prepare for next week

Weekly Planner

Monday

Tuesday

Wednesday

Thursday

Friday

Saturday

Sunday

Note

Weekly meeting

Clients to call

Things to prepare for next week

Weekly Planner

Monday

Tuesday

Wednesday

Thursday

Note

Friday

Saturday

Sunday

Weekly meeting

Clients to call

Things to prepare for next week

Weekly Planner

Monday

Tuesday

Wednesday

Thursday

Note

Friday

Saturday

Sunday

Weekly meeting

Clients to call

Things to prepare for next week

Weekly Planner

Monday

Tuesday

Wednesday

Thursday

Note

Friday

Saturday

Sunday

Weekly meeting

Clients to call

Things to prepare for next week

Weekly Planner

Monday

Tuesday

Wednesday

Thursday

Note

Friday

Saturday

Sunday

Weekly meeting

Clients to call

Things to prepare for next week

Weekly Planner

Monday

Tuesday

Wednesday

Thursday

Note

Friday

Saturday

Sunday

Weekly meeting

Clients to call

Things to prepare for next week

Weekly Planner

Monday

Tuesday

Wednesday

Thursday

Friday

Saturday

Sunday

Note

Weekly meeting

Clients to call

Things to prepare for next week

Weekly Planner

Monday

Tuesday

Wednesday

Thursday

Friday

Saturday

Sunday

Note

Weekly meeting

Clients to call

Things to prepare for next week

Weekly Planner

Monday

Tuesday

Wednesday

Thursday

Note

Friday

Saturday

Sunday

Weekly meeting

Clients to call

Things to prepare for next week

Weekly Planner

Monday

Tuesday

Wednesday

Thursday

Note

Friday

Saturday

Sunday

Weekly meeting

Clients to call

Things to prepare for next week

Weekly Planner

Monday

Tuesday

Wednesday

Thursday

Note

Friday

Saturday

Sunday

Weekly meeting

Clients to call

Things to prepare for next week

Weekly Planner

Monday

Tuesday

Wednesday

Thursday

Friday

Saturday

Sunday

Note

Weekly meeting

Clients to call

Things to prepare for next week

Weekly Planner

Monday

Tuesday

Wednesday

Thursday

Note

Friday

Saturday

Sunday

Weekly meeting

Clients to call

Things to prepare for next week

Weekly Planner

Monday

Tuesday

Wednesday

Thursday

Note

Friday

Saturday

Sunday

Weekly meeting

Clients to call

Things to prepare for next week

Weekly Planner

Monday

Tuesday

Wednesday

Thursday

Note

Friday

Saturday

Sunday

Weekly meeting

Clients to call

Things to prepare for next week

Weekly Planner

Monday

Tuesday

Wednesday

Thursday

Note

Friday

Saturday

Sunday

Weekly meeting

Clients to call

Things to prepare for next week

Weekly Planner

Monday

Tuesday

Wednesday

Thursday

Note

Friday

Saturday

Sunday

Weekly meeting

Clients to call

Things to prepare for next week

Weekly Planner

Monday

Tuesday

Wednesday

Thursday

Note

Friday

Saturday

Sunday

Weekly meeting

Clients to call

Things to prepare for next week

Weekly Planner

Monday

Tuesday

Wednesday

Thursday

Note

Friday

Saturday

Sunday

Weekly meeting

Clients to call

Things to prepare for next week

Weekly Planner

Monday

Tuesday

Wednesday

Thursday

Friday

Saturday

Sunday

Note

Weekly meeting

Clients to call

Things to prepare for next week

Weekly Planner

Monday

Tuesday

Wednesday

Thursday

Note

Friday

Saturday

Sunday

Weekly meeting

Clients to call

Things to prepare for next week

Weekly Planner

Monday

Tuesday

Wednesday

Thursday

Note

Friday

Saturday

Sunday

Weekly meeting

Clients to call

Things to prepare for next week

Weekly Planner

Monday

Tuesday

Wednesday

Thursday

Note

Friday

Saturday

Sunday

Weekly meeting

Clients to call

Things to prepare for next week

Weekly Planner

Monday

Tuesday

Wednesday

Thursday

Note

Friday

Saturday

Sunday

Weekly meeting

Clients to call

Things to prepare for next week

Weekly Planner

Monday

Tuesday

Wednesday

Thursday

Note

Friday

Saturday

Sunday

www.ingramcontent.com/pod-product-compliance
Lightning Source LLC
Chambersburg PA
CBHW081333090426
42737CB00017B/3127